Shin Yu

Pai

SIGHTINGS:

Selected

Works

(2000 - 2005)

~~Deepest please with higher~~ Special thanks
to Ferenc, David, Larry, Roland, Desiree,
Jennifer. ~~super and and editor~~ The MacDowell
Colony for providing time and support
to complete this collection.

~~_____~~
~~____~~ Book design by Murillo Design.

~~_____~~
~~____~~ Art for Unnecessary Roughness provided
courtesy of Ferenc Suto. ~~_____~~
~~_____~~ Art for Concave
is the Opposite of Convex provided courtesy
of Larry Lee. ~~_____~~
~~_____~~ Art for Nutritional Feed provided
courtesy of David Lukowski. ~~_____~~

ISBN-13: 978-0-9779351-1-6
ISBN-10: 0-9779351-1-6

1913 Press
Box 9654
Hollins University
Roanoke, Virginia 24020
www.1913press.org
editrice@journal1913.org

also
b
y

shin
yu

pai

Table of Contents

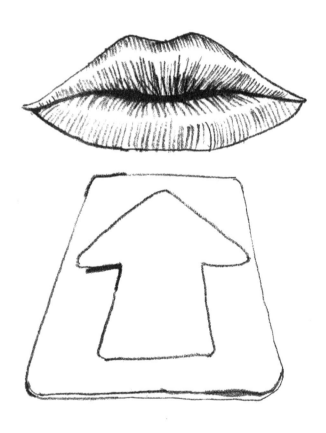

The Love Hotel Poems

c o n s o l e

				channel	lolicom		
	hello	kitty						space
		holiday				rated	gen	X
		times			five	★★★★★		familiar
			love	hotel		away	from	home

Little Chapel Christmas, Nihonbashi

decked in plastic
trees a tangle

of electric lights
girls with the I.Q.s

of potted plants
mistletoe, ornament

pediment

pedophilic

fetishists   .

Xmas comes
365 days a year

something special slipped
into a stocking

what she wants –
a Burberry scarf,

or designer handbag
pleasure in a box of

knee socks and underwear

in this Nativity scene

Jesus the name
of just another john

Hello Kitty

brand identification
                        begins at an early age

with hairpins
                & rubbers

then cell phones &
                        vibrators

the passage from girlhood
                        to woman

marked by references

                to apple and banana

                        euphemisms of deflowering

in the altered graphic

        a cherry leaf & stem replaces

                        pussy's red bow

        as she nurses a digit

                        round-faced cat

                        without a mouth

what would you say you have seen

smiling rabbits looking on

Trojan Horse

sometimes she dreamed of bits
as women dream of jewelry

an oiled line of bridle straps
the weight of a shining piece

what crushed Catherine the Great's
reign, mythic as Greek warriors

emptying quietly into the night

hello, nurse!

falling under
        the scope of practice

chiropractic services,
        fashion health
            massage
               & rejuvenating facials

for fascia, deep tissue
        bone repositioning

manipulated articulations &
        maneuvering of the lower extremities

providing on-site delivery:
        otaku,
          (your "venerable house")
              or mine?

kogals   kegels   cosplay

How delightful everything is!
    or Things that are dispensed from vending machines

Hamburgers, hot dogs, and takoyaki.

Beer, sake, whiskey and milk.

Hooks and fishing bait.

D, C, and AA sized batteries.

Video games, vibrators, disposable cameras, and film.

Soiled schoolgirls' panties.

Toilet paper.

Omikuji*.

Live beetles. Rhinoceros and stag are especially popular for breeding or as pets.

Rice by the kilo.

Fresh vegetables picked this morning.

Breaded chicken, French fries, and fried sea bream.

*strips of paper used for fortune telling sold at Shinto shrines

p r o v i s i o n (a l)

ice cream that never melts:
      whipped potatoes
            under chocolate sauce

rice noodles
          dressed in ketchup
             served with spoon & fork –

                            (the demise of slurping)
    trompe l'oeil

school girls in uniform
             & wide-eyed gaijin

      hunt through Kappabashi District

plastic manufactured
        food
           kowtowing

    to the West

the American palate
        in 3 dimensions:
           hamburger, hot dog, BLT

human beings are visual
         learners,
            things are rarely what they seem

displayed under glass
        cool fluorescent hum
          fills a simulated silence

STAR FLEET LOG

on board the flight
        of the challenger

Western theories
        do not fly

men are from Mars

      and women are from Venus

& Asian male penis
        size does matter

as much as
       a man's salary

falling beneath
       the national average

      abandon all hope
         of full sensor scans
            mind melds
             &glow-
               in the dark condoms

in the old reruns (the search for Spock)
      outfitted in skin-tight uniform
         Lt. Sulu is quoted
as saying

    "Don't call me tiny."

Love Train

white-gloved working stiffs
shove riders into openings
cars at 160% capacity
       on the morning commute
 salarymen stand
            accused of groping
office ladies
      flowers of the workplace
schoolgirls young
      as a neighbor's daughter
hang on nylon straps
        bouncing to
          the train's rhythmic
     method
       pulling out
        of the station
the press of bodies
      tamaranai – an uncontrollable urge
enough cause
     for arrest & conviction
paying off the yakuza
     and other authorities
     for a falsely I.D.ed
         positive
       keep hands in sight
        at all times

tie me up, tie me down

the Western tradition:
      a punishment
reserved for
      petty thieves
          wife beaters
            drunkards
             &   fortune-tellers
unforetold perversions
      in the land of the rising sun:
          a feudal obsession with sex
     stocks and bonds
            paired and cropped
             crotch shot
a photographer with rope describes it
             to the press
since I can't tie up their hearts, I tie up their bodies
masturbatory
      printed matter
          shoved into
          a tight corner
imagine an adulterer
      tethered
          to a pole/ buried
          to the neck
one hundred villagers
      discharging across
          his/her deathlike mask

Notes From a Love Hotel Diary
or *Sugitaru Wa Oyobazaru Ga Gotoshi

Picked up on the internet. 6.5 emails. Invited her here after a sporting event. She had a baby face, but she had a really hot body. She was a D-Cup and had a really slender waist. She gave me a good blowjob too. I think she's a keeper, at least for now. She got really wet while we were just kissing. Two hours later, she put on her school uniform and road home on her bike.

Recently not one single good thing has happened to me. The sex is lousy too. I don't even masturbate. I hate being 19 years old and in this situation. I want to meet someone I can be happy with ALL my friends have boyfriends. I've got to find someone!

You and your wife can do whatever you want inside the suite and no one can hear either of you scream.

I owe a lot to this hotel, I've come here with my boyfriend about 20 times, and when we have a fight, I come here alone to get out of the house. I come here a lot, and I'D probably come here again.

Wish they had these in America!

Happiness is possible, even when your partner is someone else's husband.

* sometimes too little is better than too much

Dirty

in the aftermath of love-

making the bed, stripping
sweat-soaked sheets

the unmentionable

details of a family
owned operation,

an obasan sanitizes
the spanking horse

while a granddaughter
tidies rooms, rows

of empty spines

behind the scenes
a pair of liver-spotted

hands taking a key

Unnecessary
Roughness

square it up

to a fresh
fish

b
o
b
b l
e

chicken
feet
Pelé
f
i
s
t j r
i e

2 4
3 1

on the fly
e
l n
j
a i
e
K

ri
a c
l beami n --- j
t buck
o
o
n

o
u
t

y - e#@!schulzed!@#
s
it up P
a
s
s
i
n

serving
bitch

DODGEBALL

shirts vs. skins

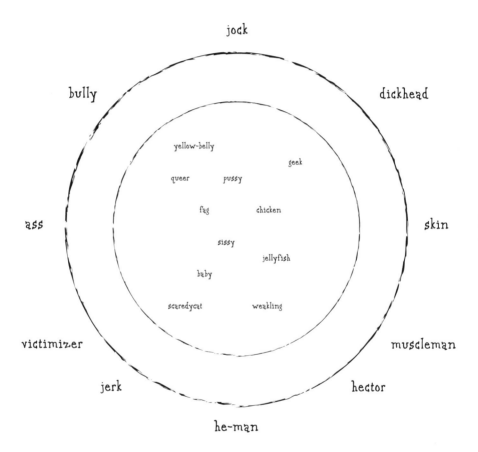

jock

bully　　　　　　　　　　　dickhead

yellow-belly

geek

queer　　pussy

fag　　　chicken

ass　　　　　　sissy　　　　　　skin

jellyfish

baby

scaredycat　　weakling

victimizer　　　　　　　　muscleman

jerk　　　　　　　　hector

he-man

since the gay

old days of

this country

the American pastime

of manhandling

the opponent

taking down

to the ground

the player

holding the ball

S   M   E   A   R   I   N   G

T H E   Q U E E R

P.E.

there is something
for everyone and for
everyone else
there is

running or jumping
in place a basic
knowledge of the body's
locker room

unlettered sweatshirts
and white crew socks
rubber shoes and rubber
pants'ed again, show

your school spirit or
just your undergarments
soiling the parquet floor
of the gymnasium

on a rainy day,
the school colors are drab
grey as any prefab notion of
taught "fitness"

a sense of team or
tribe, it's cannibals
and rats who delight
in eating their own

last one
picked

band practice

stars and stripes forever
a *bandfag*, the yellow
stripe of cowardice

running down
your back feel
the turfburn

against a field
of stars all
pomp and circum-

stance of a drum
major, away games
and make out sessions

on the bus
players and cheer
squad come divided

skinny geeks
transformed into more
awkward pansies

a pageant of roses

stars of track and field

the lower half of the body
should do all the work

no jumping nor jostling,
head held at horizontal

no vertical bob of
blowjobs, breathing

through the nose not
mouth, no right

way to breathe but a
better way to run with

the team long distance
endurance, soloing

the cleanest high
first orgasm

smells like teen spirit

picking up girls is
one of many perks

aerial maneuvers
and heavy lifting

hands on hips
go or punch

bow and arrow
shooting daggers

behind the bleachers
the free form splay,

pleated minis and
perky majorettes

leading the cheer
fluff them

pom poms
and perfect

your herkie
the "hurdler",

side and front
twiddling

streaming
chrome batons

and round and round it goes...

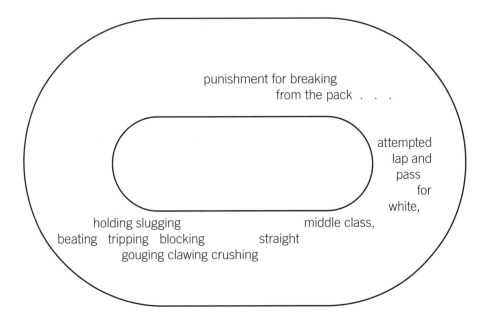

punishment for breaking
from the pack .   .   .

attempted
lap and
pass
for
white,

holding slugging
beating   tripping   blocking
gouging clawing crushing

middle class,

straight

Offensive Play

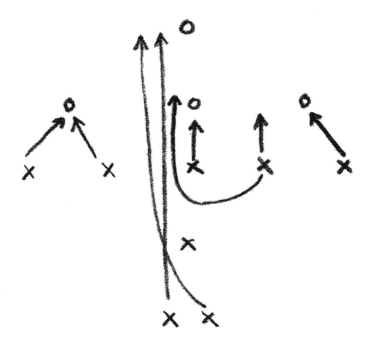

breakfast of champions

egged on
by the public
that guy owes
me some bacon
served up over
easy with a side
of milquetoast
buttered and laid
in a dish of milk
the one who speaks
softly, gets
whacked
first, with
a big stick

two minute minor (warm-up)

instant	illegal
replay	blocking
all	unnecessary
star	roughness
trophy	play
boys	the
and	hook
girls	rule
take	book
a hit	tripping
for	penalty
the	boxing
team	cauliflower ear

rookie

play pitcher
or catcher
take popshots
than hit
the showers
drill and suit
up for more
push-up
bras and
athletic supporters
fitting in
uniform
off sides
everyone's a winner

on the secret sex lives of body builders

hard on yourself
and hard on others

the cock isn't
a muscle that
grows in proportion...

to a man's ego
I went out there
feeling like King Kong

atop the Chrysler tower,
the heroine was heavy -
by building standards

she can weigh 150
pounds, I don't care
if she's a good fuck

having chicks around
is the kind of thing that
breaks up intense

training

everyone jump on
and we'll all
get together

oui
we

the pursuit of masculine perfection

one pump is
better than coming
up a disciplined,
young savage
strapping yet brutal
in white leather
inversion
boots

fit and well
hung he
could tell you squat
about submission
banished from
the competition
for unnecessary
roughness
at break time
league expansion,
everywhere

legs
legs
legs

wrestlemania

there is no chance
of points until

you've got him
off his feet

flat on
his face but

you want him
flat on

his back
taking the

bump, getting
stuffed with

a crowbar, for
the takedown

the high crotch lift
lock arms around

thigh and

heave

ice ice baby

assume the "ready"
position – target practice

for the opposition

pass-out play behind
the net, drop and smother

anything he can catch
he can control

a standing goal-tender
preferred to one who

flops to stop
going down

on bent knees

```
                  in                              option
                  every                             of
                  heat                            group

     laps

                                                   and


                  latex          smooth                     solo
                  rubber         chested
                        caps
     and                unrolled                           medley
                        over
                        heads




                        clean
                        shaven








                                  stream-
                                  lining




     flips
```

five minute major

no	kneeing	slash	punching	grand
pain	groin	and	sack	slam
no	bite	burn	hooker	holding
gain	points	on	whistle	score
for	pain	choking	blow	bodycheck
insubordination	fouling	performance	penalty	kick

career ending injuries

puck to the eye

subdural hematoma

spinal cord concussion

second impact syndrome

brain swelling

aneurysm

paralysis

fractured cervical vertebrae

a blade to the throat

baseball bat to the knee

repeated kicks to groin

Concave is the Opposite of Convex, installation view, 2000

Concave is the Opposite of Convex, installation view, 2000

Concave is the Opposite of Convex, video still "Wells, Fargo", 2000

Concave is the Opposite of Convex, installation view, 2000

Concave is the Opposite of Convex, video still "Wells, Fargo", 2000

Concave is the Opposite of Convex, video still "Wells, Fargo", 2000

Concave is
the Opposite
of Convex

Concave is the Opposite of Convex

(or lines from a Chinese – English phrase book)

A PLAY FOR 4 VOICES

The Characters

VOICE 1:   **WELLS FARGO**

VOICE 2:   **SAM WONG**

VOICE 3:   **SAM'S ASSISTANT**

VOICE 4:   **JUDGE**

SCENE 1

           (Sam Wong enters.)

SAM WONG: I came because it was convenient.

I came at the first opportunity.

It suits me to come.

I do so because I love to.

I came for I had a splendid chance.

I came for I had a good chance.

Well! I thought I would drop in while passing.

Well! I thought I would make a visit while passing.

Well! I thought I would step in while passing by here.

Well! I thought I would step in for a moment.

Oh! I came because I had nothing to do at home.

(Enter Wells Fargo and Sam's Assistant to conduct business transaction.)

WELLS FARGO: The house was set on fire by an incendiary.

SAM WONG: I will rent the house if you include the water.

SAM'S ASSISTANT: I will attach his furniture if you idemnify me.

SAM WONG: Please tell me what is the name of my landlord?

SAM'S ASSISTANT: (Whispered into Sam Wong's ear.)
I collect the bills.

SAM WONG: Are you sure of it?

SAM'S ASSISTANT: Certainly, it is true.

He is a tax collector.

He is a money collector.

WELLS FARGO: I don't cheat, even a boy.

SAM WONG: What is your honorable surname?

SAM'S ASSISTANT: (Aside) Permanent Employment.

(Wells Fargo exits stage.)

SAM'S ASSISTANT: What did you dislike in him?

SAM WONG: He was intending to afflict me by telling me fibs.

SAM'S ASSISTANT: Why did you dislike him?

SAM WONG: He squatted on my lot.

SAM'S ASSISTANT: He believed his testimony.

SAM WONG: He claimed my mine.

SAM'S ASSISTANT: He was once a stationer.

SAM WONG: He was much disgraced.
The judge will certainly convict him
He was convicted by the jury.
He is now a convict.

SAM'S ASSISTANT: In what court?

SAM WONG: "You do things without a cause."

In the Court of You Do Things without a Just Cause

JUDGE: Well, sir! What do you want? *Bangs gavel.*

WELLS FARGO: I have made an apology, but still he wants to strike me.

SAM WONG: I will expel him if he don't leave the place.

JUDGE: *(Shouting)* Can you wait a few days longer?

SAM WONG: I buy goods from you, I want you to deliver them to my place.

JUDGE: He has to hire a very good lawyer to defend himself.

SAM'S ASSISTANT: Because his crime was so great.

JUDGE: Did they find anything in his possession?

SAM'S ASSISTANT: He cut a man's hand off by an accident.

WELLS FARGO: Collectively speaking, they were few.

JUDGE: Did his witness give a good evidence?

SAM'S ASSISTANT: The teacher modified the sentence.

SAM WONG: How much will you charge to guarantee that there?

JUDGE: What will be the charges per month for a vegetable dealer and his two baskets to Oakland and return daily.

SCENE 3

SAM WONG: On what day is it possible for you to depart?

WELLS FARGO: The steamer will depart tomorrow.

SAM WONG: When will you be ready?

WELLS FARGO: On board the vessel.

SAM'S ASSISTANT: The immigration from Europe to New England has been very large since the war was over.

SAM WONG: All aboard.

SAM'S ASSISTANT: Boston is the capital of Massachusetts.

WELLS FARGO: Good-bye; I must go home now.

SAM WONG: Very well, I thank you.

(Wells Fargo exits stage opposite from Sam Wong and Sam's Assistant.)

FIN

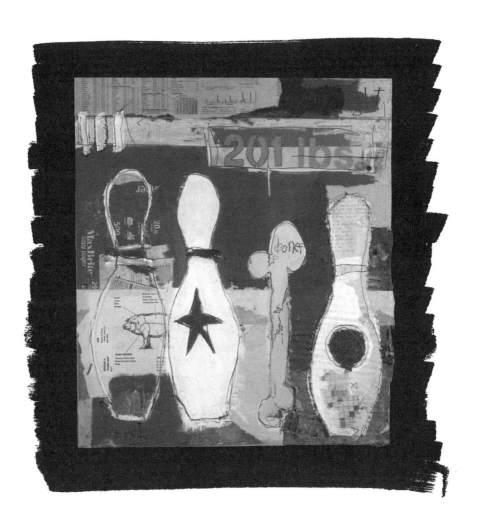

Found the Pocket [Lucky Strike], 2004

Nutritional Feed

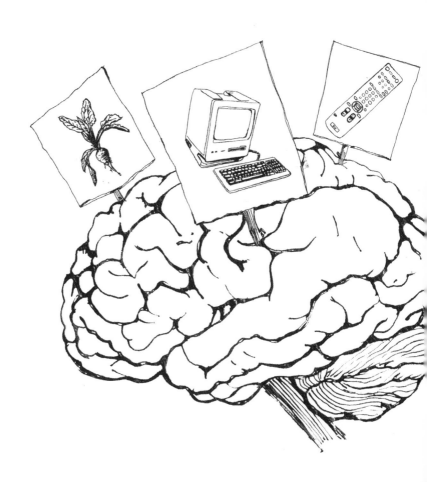

figuratively speaking

IT'S ALL WHITE MEAT

the archetypal
      "good pig" or
              chicken
     kielbasa links
          to heart disease,
              high blood pressure
                  cooked well-
done lean prime cut
      priced to sell
          before expiration

usda approved
          standards
            of living
              wage wars over

            nutritional feed

             occluded heart

                    &

                     embolism

it does a body good

the

food   pyramid

was not **3 - 5** built

by   **SERVINGS IN A DAY** M.D.s

or nutrition experts but the agricultural industry

HOOD®ed promotions
from the dairy farmers
of America

build strong teeth
&
bones,
grow
lactose
intolerance

flatulence
& the runs

GOT MILK?

(of magnesia)

in 1927
> recognized symbols
>> for **GENERAL** FOODS:

a heart   5¢
> five cents
>> a smiling face

American EYE-con
of the mid-west
smiling limbless
brain box packet
man savior

feel   **phantom pain?**

(combine 2 cups sugar: 1 gallon water: 1 packet artificial drink mix)

elect from

the following:

grape

lemon-lime

cherry

orange

raspberry

strawberry

(omit sugar and increase pre-packaged mix for known alternative uses)

hairdye

OH YEAH   woodstain

dish cleaner

heads up! (7up)

nap time   quiet time   no more questions

      close eyes   &   follow directions

thumb suck obedience school

      game-play elimination

      stand up & void

      socialize acculturate indoctrinate rules

      stop drop & roll

        or duck & cover
           the brain-
             case split

      between **education
    & learning**

      oppositional tones
        on the master palette

(COLORBLINDED)

      canvas still life

         GREEN EGGS w/HAM

shows a picture

with heart,

organ

sonagram

meat

served as

Packaged Nutritional

Facts: Caloric

Units

of Heat

Raise

The Temperature   **Within**

The Walls of   **The Heart**

Ascending

Descending

Muscles, Game   **Play**

The Red Suit

Is Avoided/Consumed   **In**

As Recommended   Perform

Quadruple   **Bypass**

To Avoid
Obstruction

The Taste
of Rawness   •   Weighed

Against Feathers

rung   & riser

terrapin   ladder

climber   starfuck   aspirations

towards   alpinism   the   king

of all I see - chicken of the

sea   tuna   melt   mercury

poisoning   New   York   Times

reports   the   voice   of   America

says *sorry Charlie* we're   not

fooled   by   abstract   painting,

dance   or   poetry,   *we want tuna*

that tastes great, not   tuna w/

great   *taste*

```
                    USER AUTHENTICATION
        NAME:   NET
    PASSWORD:   COOKIE
```

open dialogue
               box
                    reads
                    "generating error log" (x 55)

[virus infects & multiplies] – – – – – – – – – – – – – – – –

                         specified server
                               no longer exists

                    no device available – – – – – – – – – –

          can't back-up. undo?

       hold for tech support

               Subject: ticket request #4123894798

                    please ping me

          Re: systems outage

                    all available resources are at work
                              on the problem

                                             command quit ALL

                                             clear history

                                        next
                                        time
                                               track

                                             document
                                             all changes

operate

telephone

operative

teleplay

operations

teletext

operatic

telephony

operator

telecom

unskilled
labor over
incremental
increases
graded
professional
development

tiered

rewards

system

fifteen minute
breaks dream
white - castles
in the sky

dial øut for assistance

split   X   X   X   X

impact   X   X

what's left standing

from an organized split

aim for the cluster

s
e
a
l   o f f

conquer

and

divide

candlepin

      pork

         bowl

        snooker wagers

on the pocket

       eye-hand coordination

cuestick

     eight

        - ball crack

           hot oracle

              boner in

                   the corner

                   snatch

LUCKY
STRIKE

STAT•YT

Q'TY: 6

graphic
    elements

1. cardboard
2. clasp
3. clay
4. and ochre
5. whitewashed
6. volcanic
    ash

physical system

    of quantum variables

the indirect
object
defined:

it occurs
w/out
equal

Ǝye

TEST

MULTIPLE

SPECTRUMS

SEE THROUGH

FINGER TIP'S

IMPRINT

WHERE'S MY JACKET?

the figure
vanishes

under white-out and cover-up

Houdini act:
show/hide all

suspended
in a glass box

results are always
perfect

invisible
TRANSPARENCY

sent through
the transporter
atomic information
lost and scrambled
ratio aspects

Aprilaire

```
v         v           v
 a         a           a
  p         p       p
       o   o
           r
```

exhalations

expire along

corrugated ridges

of brain

dampness

apparatus

storms↑

&

↓ drafts

turn

liquid under pressure ↵

shrinkwrap tight

to prevent leakage

at 25% humidity and dropping

the sketch begins

to fade

paint dried

solid remains

it may take you far away...

breaking
    through
        the sound barrier

intergalactical travel
        to distant places

circle

    coalsack
            nebulae

    star-gazing

VELA

                                ARA

    ALTAIR

                            VEGA

in search
        of new

        → turbo on towards

                            HOME

spaceboy, I miss you

look mom no plugs or inside the iron lung

brachiole branchiole bronchiole

boneless flank of beef
invertebrate animal anatomy
lacks a backbone

branching as
in the government
my Uncle Bill

on life support
keeps breathing thanks
to negative pressure

fed on dream rub
eraser heads
to keep clean

steel zinc manganese

normal

household

(+) battery (-)

and waste
recyclable
leakage & rupture

the circuit complete

when the power runs out
we'll just hum
a song

(clearing of throat)

      followed by

          (characteristic wheezing noises)

    OK
    OK
    OK

EYE - **Q**

&

A

ON THE MR. BUTCH SHOW

STYLIZED MONOLOGUES

AND SUITCASE SOLILOQUYS

APPEARING NOW

IN THE ALLSTON

PANHANDLE

FLAT BROKE &

HOMELESS

YOU CAN BE WHATEVER

COLOR YOU WANT

TO BE

BLUE

YELLOW

OR

EVEN GREENSPAN

(*CLOSED CAPTIONING ERROR)

bed-   *time*

story

henpecked   chicken   wire   tinfoil   antennae   channel

zero   static   blue   fuzz   safety   jacket   broadcast

emergency   system   PSAs   time-save   T.V.   dinner

hungry man mac & cheese chicken pot pie king of beers

mute volume channel surf bathroom break no remote control

I think I saw a chickenhawk

the natives are friendly

nina	pinta	santa maria
NO	STANDING	AFTER
stagflation	and	**malaise**
people	*lie*	&
chickens	*lay*	Reaganomic
rotisserie	roasted	super
hero	super	**size**

what came
first:

chicken / egg
shell & bullet

broadcast America

riddled as chalk
      & Swiss cheese
           the editorial content:
a folded boat
      would never
          buoy

though perhaps
      a paper hat

daily *HERALD*

    and **HEADLINER** news

print era in our
      nation's history

unscramble Morse
      code transmissions
          &radio frequencies

news break
      fast
          pore over
            funnies

SPY   NE

SECRET WATCHER   ATOMIC #10

PARA TU
   REVOLUCION   NEON

                                                    RED- ORANGE GLOW

SURFACE GLARES   OF TELEVISION
                                            NEWS

   DUCT TAPE
    ACTS   OF   T E R R O R   -ISM

VALENCY   CAPACITY TO

    ØØØ   UNITE
                                            REACT
                                                INTERACT

CONFLATE
INFLATE
DEFLATE

INTELLIGENCE

   NOTED

← **suck squeeze   B-A-N-G!**   b   l   o   w →

loosely sewn

     spaghetti western

story of   the good

                                      & the ugly

               the bad

misdemeanors: possession

of firearm narcotic bootleg

now serving time

in the academy

(click here to apply)

██████████ ACKNOWLEDGMENTS: I am grateful to the editors and publications who ██████ ██████████ first published texts from this book. Thanks to Poemeleon, Daschund, Boog City, Carve, moria, HOW2, O Poss, 580 Split, Admit 2, Blackbox, ██████████, The ███ Bedside Guide to No Tell Motel and Conspicuous Production: The First 2 Years of the Southside on Lamar Artist Residency.

The Love Hotel Poems were published ████████ ████████ by Press Lorentz as an artist's book in September 2006.

The poems in Unnecessary Roughness were ███ published as an e-chapbook ██████████ of the same name by xpress(ed) books in Spring 2005.

DESIGN, ILLUSTRATION AND PRODUCTION:
Murillo Design, Inc., ▓▓▓▓▓▓▓▓, San
Antonio, Texas. Rolando G. Murillo, Desiree
Yanes, ▓▓▓▓▓▓▓▓ and Jennifer Murillo.

Designed and produced using Adobe InDesign,
▓▓▓▓▓▓▓▓▓▓▓▓▓, Adobe Photoshop,
and Adobe Illustrator on Macintosh ▓▓▓▓▓
▓▓▓▓▓▓▓ computers.

Typefaces used throughout the book were
Vintage Typewriter and Trade Gothic,
▓▓▓▓▓▓▓▓▓▓▓▓▓▓▓▓▓▓▓▓▓▓
▓▓▓▓▓▓▓▓▓▓▓.

Printed by McNaughton & Gunn, Inc., Saline,
Michigan.

ABOUT THE AUTHOR: ~~████████████████████~~
~~████████████████████~~ Shin Yu Pai,
born September 28, 1975 in Decatur, IL, grew
up in the ~~████~~ Inland Empire of Southern
California. She studied at the Jack Kerouac
School of Disembodied Poetics at the Naropa
Institute and received her MFA from the School
of the Art Institute of Chicago. A practicing
~~████████████████~~ visual artist as
well as a poet, she has exhibited her work at
the Three Arts Club of Chicago, The Paterson
Museum, Harvard University, The MAC, and the
gallery at The University of Texas at Dallas.
~~████████████████████~~ she
has collaborated across disciplines with ~~███~~
composers, dancers, photographers and ~~█████~~
installation artists. Currently, she lives
in Dallas. ~~████████████████████~~
~~████████████████████~~

Visit her website at http://shinyupai.com.

AUTHOR'S NOTE: THESE TEXTS WERE WRITTEN OVER
A FIVE-YEAR PERIOD IN RESPONSE TO ARTWORK BY MISTY
KEASLER, FERENC SUTO, LARRY LEE, AND DAVID LUKOWSKI,

SHIN YU PAI
DALLAS, TEXAS
JANUARY 2007

ISBN-13: 978-0-9779351-1-6
ISBN-10: 0-9779351-1-6

51600

9 780977 935116

for

TYrone

with gratitude,

Shin Yu